STAY
CYBER SAFE

WHAT EVERY CEO SHOULD KNOW ABOUT CYBERSECURITY

JT KOSTMAN, PHD
BRIAN J. GALLAGHER, MPS

Introducing CodeLock™

Described by the U.S. Department of Homeland Security as being able to "stop the most sophisticated criminal malware." (DHS, 2021)

Stay Cyber Safe: What Every CEO Should Know About Cybersecurity

ISBN: 978-1-09836-889-0 *Paperback*

*We dedicate this book, our company,
and our professional lives to helping anyone who has ever
been bullied; on the playground, at work,
by criminals, or by people in positions of power.*

TABLE OF CONTENTS

Why Did We Write This Book and For Whom Did We Write It?

We, the authors of this book, are from two generations, but we have quite a bit in common.

We both started our professional careers as EMTs and went on to become Paramedics, then Police Officers.

We both had an affinity for computers and technology, and we both ended up in the private sector – as business executives and then as entrepreneurs and investors.

We are both driven by an ethos that has pervaded all our work; a compulsion to serve and protect. That was the impetus for founding our company, ProtectedBy.AI with goal of protecting people, property, places – and the profits of the small and midsized businesses (SMBs) that drive the U.S. and global economies.

Our company is committed to bringing the same capabilities to SMBs that the Tech Titans and Fortune 500 are now using to gain an unfair advantage and monopolize every industry.

Our mission, in short, is to help SMBs contend with the Goliathan forces allied against them by arming them with customized, cost-effective 'slingshots' – and making sure they know how to use them.

This brief book is focused on one of our key capabilities: Cybersecurity.

In the pages that follow, we will empower you by providing insights into the challenges and enemies you face, and we will offer some guidance on what you can do to keep yourself safe.

We also want you to know that this book does not end at the last page. It comes with an open and never-ending offer.

While we hope you will call on us to help you keep your company safe and/or to explore the extraordinary opportunities you can gain in improving profitability, efficiency, and additional market share through our other services at the intersection of Technology and Psychology.

Please know that you can call us anytime for advice – and those calls will never cost you a single cent.

We both hung up our uniforms many years ago, but we never surrendered our commitments to protect and to serve.

Forward

If you're like most CEOs, you probably find the topic of cybersecurity as stimulating as a warm glass of milk and an Ambien. We hear you. Heaven knows, you already have enough other stuff to worry about. Constantly increasing competition and costs, litigation and legislation that has run off the rails, customer and employee expectations that increase every day. And don't get us started on COVID.

So, why should you care about an esoteric topic you already pay your IT team to worry about? Because your company – and your professional life – depend on it. As much as you may be mindful of all the other risks you face, there are few other threats that can take your company from being comfortable to closed in a click.

**"I suppose I'll be the one
to mention the elephant in the room."**

Malware, ransomware, viruses, data theft, hacks…tune into the business press on any given day and you'll see yet another story, about yet another company, attacked by yet another kid in a hoodie halfway around the world. And yet another CEO who was forced to resign. Customers, shareholders, legislators, regulators, and reporters have become unforgiving, and they are increasingly blaming the victims of unexpected cyber-assaults.

But have no fear (okay, have some fear, just a bit less). This brief little book is going to give you the information you need to get on the path to keeping your company safe.

With an investment of just an hour or two of your time, you will come away from these pages confident in your ability to make critical tradeoff decisions on how best to safeguard your critical information and data assets. In less than the time it takes to watch a movie, you will get the essential information you need to direct your IT teams and ensure they are aligned with your protection priorities.

The insights we share here will greatly increase the odds of keeping you and your company from being featured as failed fiduciaries of data assets on CNN.

So, here's our promise: This book will give you the basics without the BS. We'll tell you what you most need to know without geek-speak, computer code or equations. We'll try to 'edutain' you a bit with interesting tidbits, brief stories, and (regrettably) bad jokes. We will ignore the academic minutia and give you practical, actionable advice on how you can immediately (and surprisingly affordably) keep your organization much safer and more secure than it is right now.

And we'll do our best to make sure we don't put you to sleep – but at the same time, we'll help you make sure you're not as cyber-exposed, so you can sleep better at night.

The Authors

Dr. JT Kostman has spent 40+ years protecting countries, companies, communities, and people. Prior to co-founding ProtectedBy.AI, he served in CXO roles with two Fortune 50 companies and as an advisor to hundreds of organizations, ranging from Silicon Valley startups to U.S. Intelligence, Defense, and Security agencies.

Brian Gallagher spent a decade working with the U.S. Secret Service before going on to a career as an internationally recognized expert on security and risk mitigation. He is the co-founder of ProtectedBy.AI, where he leads teams committed to protecting people, property, places – and profits.

1

The Times They Are a-Changin'

If you're a CEO or Senior Executive, the odds are pretty good that you grew up in very different world than the one we're all living in now. You can probably remember a time when you could change your own spark plugs and tune up your own car. Today? The engine compartment of an SUV (another thing we didn't have when we were kids) looks like a circuit board – and your car has basically become a computer on wheels.

You can probably also remember a time when you had to get off your couch and put on pants to go shopping. When a bookstore was a place where you could visit, browse and sit. When Alexa and Siri might have been the names of kids you went to school with – but they certainly weren't lurking around waiting to answer burning questions, like "Alexa, what is 42?" [Try it yourself, if you haven't already].

If you're reading this, you might remember the first time men went to the moon – and recall that they did so with computing capabilities that were vastly inferior to that smartphone you can now fit in your pocket.

If you are reading this, you can likely
remember a time before the Digital Age.

Bridging the Digital Divide

Yes, a lot has changed since we were kids. Bellbottoms are out (but tie-dye is making a comeback) and the World Wide Web is no longer just a private club where only the fortunate few with a dial-up modem and an AOL account can join in on the fun. These days you're likely connected from the moment you wake up to the minute you go to bed, and even as you drive down the road.

As the real world has increasingly moved into the cyber world, bridging the carbon/silicon divide, our lives have improved in countless ways. There are infinitely many more purchasing options for just about everything under the sun. We can connect to family and friends across the oceans for free. The days when you used to get yelled at because "they're calling long distance!" are over. Every mom-and-pop shop can now have the same sort of cyber presence as a Fortune 500 company. White collar professionals can increasingly work from anywhere – and sweatpants and flip flops have become sartorial options for those who would, at one time, have felt compelled to wear a blouse or blazer.

Danger Will Robinson!

All this newfound freedom and opportunity come with very real threats to our security. The computer and network connections – the most liberating combination of capabilities in human history – have also exposed us to hackers, state actors and cyber-criminals from everywhere on the globe.

While security threats have been with us since before the beginning of the internet, there is no denying digital challenges are accelerating – and getting much, much worse.

Those Were the Days, My Friend…

Are you old enough to remember when the World Wide Web began way back in 1991? How about when e-commerce burst onto the scene in 1998?

Were you already in the workforce when Facebook was launched, and the era of social networking began in 2004? When Cloud Computing started to make it rain money in 2006?

How about way, way back in 2013 when more than half of the adults in America reported that, for the first time, they were banking online?

And what have you been up to over the past five years as Artificial Intelligence has proven to be more of an economic disruptor than any force in history?

Let's face it. We are living in a world very different than the one most of us were born into.

And if you're not keeping up with technology, you are getting left behind.

Stay Cyber Safe: What Every CEO Needs to Know About Cybersecurity is a cautionary tale intended to provide the critical information you most need to know to save yourself sleepless nights. It is the book you will wish you had read if (when) you are hacked and find yourself having to explain to your customers, your stockholders/stakeholders and the press why you were caught off guard.

In this little book we will share a few stories to help illustrate the extent of the cyber threats you face – and the clear and present danger cyber criminals pose. Any leader of any organization today needs to be informed and aware of how to protect the digital assets of their enterprise. This must-know overview is written specifically for executives who are too busy ensuring the survival and success of their organization in today's digital marketplace to have the time or inclination to deal with technical minutiae.

2

The Rising Tide of Cyber Crime: A Brief History

Malware (a portmanteau of the words "*mali*cious" and "soft*ware*") has been a persistent and escalating challenge since the first experimental self-replicating virus, *Creeper System*, was developed by Bob Thomas at BBN Technologies in 1971.

The Worm Turns

Creeper moved among computers using the ARPANET (Advanced Research Projects Agency Network), the predecessor of the internet. While the original version simply hopped from machine to machine, advanced versions were programmed to be self-replicating – making *Creeper* the first computer worm. Unlike its poisonous progeny that threatens us today, Creeper was harmless and caused no damage to data or systems. Its only purpose was to play a digital version of "tag, you're it!" by printing a message through the teletype attached to infected systems that read, "I'm the creeper: catch me if you can."

"The hospital computer system has a virus.
Ironic, isn't it?"

The first computer virus to be released in the wild – *Brain* – was developed by Amjad Farooq Alvi and Basit Farooq Alvi in 1986. Brain was ostensibly created to stop people from pirating medical software the Alvi brothers had developed – and it proved to be as effective as it was infuriating.

Unless users entered a valid license number, *Brain* overrode the boot sector of the floppy disks of the computers of those who had purloined the Alvi's program. *Brain* then issued a cryptic message, "Welcome to the Dungeon" and a warning, "Beware of this VIRUS ... Contact us for a vaccination," along with contact information for obtaining a valid license to use the program. The ability to effectively hold a computer hostage made Brain the first piece of ransomware – a threat that has caused incalculable damage over the past few years.

The Rise of Ransomware

On June 27, 2017, an IT support technician working at the head-quarters of A.P. Møller-Maersk received an ominous message on his computer: "opps, your important files are encrypted".

The price to decrypt those files: $300 worth of bitcoin.

Annoying, of course. But $300? Such a trivial amount was not worth fretting about. Pay the ransom and get on with your day.

If only it had been that simple.

The ransom was a ruse and only led to further infections. By the time the NotPetya ransomware virus ran its course, it cost com-panies – including Maersk, Merck, Mondelēz, FedEx, and Reckitt Benckiser – a collective $10 billion (USD).

Over the past few years, ransomware has become so rampant and prevalent among SMBs that most (perhaps all) cybersecurity pro-fessionals have come to agree: It's no longer a matter of if you will be hit, but when.

Going Viral

The first computer virus to spread extensively was developed in 1988 by Robert Morris, a graduate student from Cornell University. *The Morris* worm was initially intended as a simple reconnaissance tool to determine the size of the internet. It was programmed by Morris to spread virally by exploiting weak passwords and security holes in Unix applications.

While not intended to serve a malevolent purpose, a small program-ming error caused the virus to spread far faster and more broadly than

Morris had intended. Within 15 hours of its release, *The Morris* infected over 15,000 computers, which in 1988 was most of the internet.

Frightening Facts

- The global impact of cybercrime is expected to reach $10.5 trillion annually by 2025.

- By 2022 there will be 3.5 million unfilled cybersecurity positions globally.

- The ten biggest data breaches in history have occurred over the past five years.

- 76 percent of U.S. companies reported having been compromised by at least one cyber-attack within the past year.

- Companies take on average over six months (197 days) to notice a data breach.

- The average company with 1,000+ employees spends $9MM/year on cybersecurity.

Birth of a Criminal Nation

The explosive growth of malware (e.g., viruses, ransomware, adware and other types of unwanted code) over the ensuing years has led to the dangerous circumstances we find ourselves in today: confronting a nearly unchecked plague of cybercrime that, as of 2021, is costing the global economy approximately $6 trillion annually. To put that into context, the gross domestic product (GDP) of the world's three leading economies, the United States, China, and Japan, are, respectively, $19.48 trillion, $12.23 trillion, and $4.87 trillion (USD). By these measures, cybercrime is now the world's third largest economy.

With few prosecutions and minimal recourse against hackers (who can access systems from anywhere in the world), and cyber-criminal paydays that routinely run to millions of dollars, it's small wonder why cybercrime has quickly become big business. *And cousin, business is a-boomin'!*

"Today, you're going to spend less time breaking into the school back office website, redirecting air traffic, sending encrypted messages overseas … and more time working on the lesson."

Cyber Tsunami

In the post-pandemic era, with the increasing global impact of economic contractions; limited legitimate opportunities for digitally savvy unemployed bored kids; increased access to hacking information and education; the near universal ubiquity of hacking tools and technology; these combined factors have contributed to create a perfect storm that is quickly coalescing into a cyber-assault tsunami.

The questions every CEO and Senior Executive in every industry are now forced to ask:

- What is your cybersecurity plan?
- Who is deciding on the cybersecurity tradeoffs you must make?
- Who needs access to what – and who do you trust?

The Security Seesaw

Cybersecurity is all about the tradeoffs you decide to make between security and accessibility. The essential question you have to ask yourself is: How much security you are willing to give up making your data more accessible, and to whom?

It is, in fact, possible to keep all your data completely secure. All you have to do is take the machine that the data is created on and store it in an inaccessible, access controlled, secured bunker – then never, ever, allow that machine to be connected to any internal or external networks -- and thoroughly search anyone who comes in contact with the machine. Of course, to be extra safe, the person interacting with the machine should also remain locked in the bunker, without being given access to anyone. Simple – though probably logistically (and legally) challenging.

The balance you have to strike is how much of your data should be made available to whom – and what steps you can prudently and practically take to ensure only that amount of access is granted.

At the end of the day, your decisions need to ensure the right people have access to the right information at the right time. And those are, unfortunately, decisions that you cannot abrogate to anyone else; not even your own CIO, CTO or CISO.

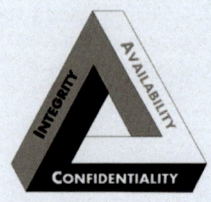

The tech-leaders in your company may fret about tradeoffs from the perspective of what is known as the 'CIA Triad' – the balance that must be maintained between the Confidentiality, Integrity, and Availability of data. But when it comes to the ultimate decisions between security and accessibility that can determine the fate of the organization…as the Bard said, "Uneasy lies the head that wears a crown."

3

Something Wicked This Way Comes

Cyberattacks have three fundamental goals: Extraction, Obstruction, Insertion.

Extraction

Extraction cyberattacks are focused on theft. The unauthorized removal of data from targeted systems. When the press reports on companies having been "hacked," this is the form of cyberattack they typically mean. Extraction cyberattacks use the internet as an access mechanism – a Window (pardon the pun) that thieves crawl through to steal digital assets (i.e., data).

The Adobe hack of October 2013 that resulted in the theft of 153 million user records? The Equifax breach of July 2017 that resulted in the theft of the personal data of 147.9 million consumers? The Bangladesh Cyber Heist of February 2016 that netted thieves $101 million (USD)? Those were extraction attacks.

Obstruction

Obstruction cyberattacks are somewhere along a continuum of merely mischievous to maliciously malevolent. These include Distributed Denial of Service (DDoS) attacks that disrupt normal traffic to a website and Man-in-the-Middle (MitM) attacks in which the hacker attacker is easily able to intercept communication between two parties, either to secretly eavesdrop or to modify the traffic traveling between A and B. Most often these sorts of assaults are merely annoying, but obstruction attacks can, in some cases, have a devastating impact on organizations.

Case in point: In February 2020, Amazon Web Services (AWS) was forced to defend itself against a 2.3 terabit-per-second (Tbps) distributed denial of service (DDoS) attack that would have crippled any other company [Geek to English Dictionary: a frickin' huge attack!]. So-called hacktivists, cyber-anarchists, and digital vigilantes are increasingly using obstruction attacks to disrupt the online operations of companies, communities, and countries.

Insertion

Insertion cyberattacks tend to be the most insidious and damaging of the three. These assaults include the unlawful and/or vastly unwelcome introduction of a variety of malware programs, including viruses, worms, spyware, Trojan horses, and more mundanely, adware. In an insertion attack, cyber-criminals inject their own computer code into the targeted victim's machine in furtherance of their nefarious purpose. The intended objective of the malware these black-hat hackers introduce is to control some or all of the functions of the targeted victim machine. Insertion attacks can often escalate into extraction attacks or massive obstruction attacks by hijacking innocent machines and turning them into "zombies" (a computer connected to the internet that has been compromised by a hacker, computer virus or Trojan horse program and can be used to perform malicious tasks of one sort or another under remote direction).

What makes insertions the most loathed of cyber-assaults is the fact that, in addition to being the most common mechanism for initiating the other two types of attacks (extraction and obstruction), insertion attacks tend to go beyond infecting the targeted systems. Their purpose is to metastasize and continue to cause damage.

Wolves in Sheep's Clothing

There's something wrong with your bank account! To keep crooks from stealing all your money, log into your account right now: www. BonkofAmerica.com

Did you catch that? Because if not, you might get Bonked.

One of the nastier tactics hackers use is referred to as "spoofing" – pretending to be someone or something they are not to gain your confidence and get access to your computers and networks.

By sending prospective victims links to websites that are either simi-lar to ones their targets might trust, or by hijacking the URL of genu-ine sites, these cyber-thieves get unsuspecting people to click – and then direct you to "change your password" by entering your current password and personal information first.

Not only do these cyber-thieves then have access to that account, but they also capitalize on the fact that most of us have only a few usernames and passwords we use for everything.

Be honest… How many websites do you use the same password for? Consider this: If you use that password on more than one site, all a bad guy has to do is get your password once, and he's instantly able to access to every website and system you use that same password for.

And if that's not bad enough, hackers now trade the information they collect the way we used to trade baseball cards when we were kids. The result? A thriving black market on the Dark Web where, for a few pennies a piece, thieves can purchase everything they need to know about you to connect the dots and take over your online life.

To make matters even worse: There is a continuously updated list on the Dark Web of the passwords that people use most com-monly. Like [CompanyName]123 – which was the password used by an intern at SolarWinds that enabled that hacker to get in.

Holding Data Hostage

Ransomware, a digital plague that has exploded in recent years, is a form of insertion attack. These pernicious, parasitic programs have not only proven to be the most successful form of cybercrime but are also now the most prevalent.

In 2016, research firm Vanson Bourne conducted a global survey of 500 cybersecurity decision makers at organizations with more than 1,000 employees and found, "In the last 12 months, 48 percent of organizations across the globe have fallen victim to a ransomware campaign, with 80 percent indicating that they've suffered from three or more attacks." The near unanimous consensus among cybersecurity experts is that ransomware has increased significantly over the past five years since that study was conducted. We are likely looking at the tipping point of an impending ransomware epidemic that will make attacks over the past few years look like little more than an annoyance.

Paving the Road to Hell

Ratcheting up the risk? Cybercrime is increasingly becoming organized and many of the hacks of private companies now originate with state actors. Russia, China, Iran, and North Korea have all gotten in on the game for gain, as well as to simply rattle capitalist cages.

In response to the release of a (truly terrible!) movie called *The Interview* – a "comedy" about a fictional plot to assassinate North Korean leader Kim Jong-un, a hacker group calling itself *Guardians of Peace* leaked a release of confidential data from film studio Sony Pictures on November 24, 2014. The data included personal information about Sony Pictures employees and their families, emails between employees, information about executive salaries at the company, copies of then-unreleased Sony films, plans and scripts for future films and troves of additional compromising information. To add injury to insult, the perpetrators added an intrusion attack to their extraction attack by embedding a variant of the *Shamoon Wiper* virus that erased Sony's entire computer infrastructure.

Russia, Iran, and China have each sponsored hack attacks of major companies in the United States as industrial espionage. So-called "hacktivists" and self-anointed "freedom of information" activists – from Anonymous to Edward Snowden – have done irreparable damage to organizations ranging from small startups to the United States government.

Chocolate, Vanilla, Rocky Road

Cyber-attacks come in three flavors, each of which is a recipe for disaster.

- **Extraction Attacks:** Bad guys take stuff out of your systems.

- **Obstruction Attacks:** Bad guys interfere with information sent from Point A to Point B.

- **Insertion Attacks:** Bad guys burrow into your computer and networks to implant cyber cancers that metastasize.

4

Winter Is Coming

The Economist, reports, "The world's most valuable resource is no longer oil, but data." And nearly every company is now data driven. CRM, ERP, HRIS, financial systems, email, and electronic files. Every aspect of the enterprise has been digitized – and the loss, corruption, or disclosure of that data can be devastating.

Legislating Security

As formidable as the forces facing organizations are from criminal hackers, senior executives and board members are finding the most significant data-related challenges they face are coming from a spate of new data-related rules, regulations, legislation and laws that can occasion draconian penalties:

- GDPR (General Data Protection Regulation) violations can occasion fines of up to €20 million, or four percent of annual worldwide revenue of the preceding financial year, whichever is greater.

- The California Consumer Privacy Act (CCPA) applies to any company that has collected data on more than 50,000 California citizens or has more than $25 million in gross revenue. The CCPA carries fines of up to $7,500 per customer record for non-compliance.

- HIPAA (Health Insurance Portability and Accountability Act) violations can result in civil penalties of up to $250,000 per incident and up to 10 years in prison.

- The GLBA (Gramm-Leach-Bliley Act), also known as the Financial Modernization Act of 1999 (15 USC §§6801-6809), requires financial institutions to explain how they share and protect their customers' private information. Penalties for non-compliance can include fines of up to $100,000 per violation, with fines for officers and directors of up to $10,000 per violation, along with criminal penalties that carry sentences of up to five years in prison and the revocation of licenses.

- The SEC Statement and Guidance on Public Company Cybersecurity Disclosures now mandates compliance with cybersecurity standards by all publicly traded companies. Penalties are unspecified and are left up to the discretion of the historically forgiving and good-natured folks at the SEC.

- The Children's Online Privacy Protection Act of 1998 (COPPA) (15 U.S.C. §§ 6501–6506) imposes specific requirements on operators of websites or online services directed to children under 13 years of age, and on operators of other websites or online services that have actual knowledge that they are collecting personal information online from a child under 13 years of age. Fines for non-compliance and violations are determined by the Federal Trade Commission (FTC) and were recently increased to up to $43,280 per privacy violation, per child.

- The Massachusetts Standards for the Protection of Personal Information of Residents of the Commonwealth (MGL 93H, 201 CMR 17.00) requires any companies or persons who store or use personal information about a Massachusetts resident to develop a written, regularly audited plan to protect personal information. A civil penalty of $5,000 may be levied for each violation and businesses can be subject to a fine of up to $50,000 for each instance of improper data disposal.

- The NYDFS Cybersecurity Regulation (23 NYCRR 500) is a new set of regulations from the NY Department of Financial Services (NYDFS) that imposes cybersecurity requirements on all covered financial institutions. Penalties for violations will be determined by NYDFS on a case-by-case basis.

- Senator Ron Wyden (D-OR) has proposed legislation that would result in jail time for CEOs found to be negligent in their duties as data fiduciaries.

Given the current political climate, and growing antipathy toward the Tech Titans of Silicon Valley, it is reasonable to expect data and privacy related legislation, regulations, and fines will likely increase significantly over the next few years.

A Step-By-Step Guide to Cybersecurity Success

To ensure you secure your cyber-assets and keep your company safe, we recommend an approach that adheres to the Cybersecurity Framework developed by the U.S. National Institute of Standard and Technology (NIST).

It is not a question of if you will be attacked – but when.

IDENTIFY

Albert Einstein was once asked what he would do if he had just an hour to save the word. His response? "I would spend the first fifty minutes trying to understand the problem."

The first step in developing a cybersecurity strategy is to decide on your priorities and assess your vulnerabilities.

The questions to consider include:

- Who should have access to what information?

- What rules, regulations, standards, and laws are you required to adhere to?

- What are your current resources and what are the capabilities of your IT team?

- What would the costs be of a breach of varying degrees?

- What information do you need to protect?

- What will the ROI be for investments in protection from different possibilities (and inevitabilities)?

A Cyber Risk Analysis and Assessment is your first step to ensuring your data protection goals are aligned with your strategy, the expectations of your organization, the talent of your team, and your corporate culture.

PROTECT

Cyber safety is about finding a balance. On one side of the scale, you can give complete access to all your systems and data to all your employees, customers, and partners. On the other side of the scale, you can lock up all your data in an impenetrable vault that not even you can gain access to. Optimizing access and ensuring security simultaneously is about putting sufficient safeguards in place to be sure your technologies and policies meet both your business and security needs.

The questions to ask your IT team include:

- Can we provide uninterrupted delivery of our services?

- Are our critical infrastructure capabilities safe?

- Can we ensure continuous support for internal operations?

- Are our backups sufficient to ensure we cannot be held hostage by ransomware?

- Can we detect the actions of intruders before major damage is done?

A Security Audit by a qualified third-party can help disclose deficiencies and deficits. And if you really want to sleep more soundly, hiring a White Hat Hacker to stress test your security is one of the best investments you can make. The one-two punch of a Security Audit and Penetration Test are a low-cost way to expose vulnerabilities and find insufficiencies in your security before the bad guys have a chance to do it for you.

DETECT

Detection is about disclosing and mitigating damage to limit the impact of extraction, obstruction, and intrusion attacks.

- The questions to ask your IT team include:
- How often are we being attacked and by whom?
- What is the process for sequestering infected or impacted nodes, so the entire network is not harmed?
- Does our Security Information and Event Management (SIEM) system collect data from multiple devices on our network?
- Do we have a Managed Endpoint Detection solution that assists in preventing cyberattacks?
- Would we benefit by incorporating Artificial Intelligence into our threat assessment, mitigation, and prevention engines to optimize our capabilities?

The most important question you can ask: What are the capabilities and costs of our Security Operations Center – and would we be better off outsourcing those services?

RESPOND

Every system, no matter how secure, can be hacked. The real measure is what you can do to keep substantial damage from being done once you have been attacked.

- What is our response plan?

- What are the duties of each member of our Incident Response Team?

- Who gets notified of what incidences, and when?

- Is there a plan in place for communicating with all affected stakeholders?

- Has our most sensitive data been encrypted so we don't have to worry about having it exploited or exposed?

- Should we, are we, using CodeLock™ to detect intrusions as soon as they occur?

The seconds, minutes, hours, and days after an attack are when you are truly tested. Taking the time to figure out what you will do when hackers attack is one of the best investments you can make. Remember: When did Noah build the ark? Before the rain.

RECOVER

Success is all about getting knocked down eight times and getting up nine. In many ways the real measure of your security efforts will be judged by how well you can recover.

The questions to consider include:

- How quickly can we return to normal operations – and what are the financial implications of restoring more quickly or slowly?

- How do we repopulate stolen or corrupted data – and how can we be sure we are not merely reinfecting ourselves?

- Have we arranged to have clean computers available for critical and key personnel?

- How do we know our systems are safe and won't just be hit again once we are back up and running?

As you consider what you will do to recover, it is worth considering: rather than just planning on how you will lock the barn door after the horse has already escaped...are there lower cost investments you can make now, rather than paying a premium once the damage is done?

5

May You Live in Interesting Times

The challenges posed by insufficient cybersecurity recently hit home for the U.S. government and thousands of companies in an attack that will likely continue to reverberate for years.

On December 14, 2020, Reuters was the first to report on what has proven to be the most damaging insertion cyberattack in history. FireEye, a California based cybersecurity company, detected a problem with a product provided by SolarWinds – a provider of information technology (IT) monitoring and management tools for System Administrators and Network Engineers.

Frontal Assault

With a customer base of at least 18,000 companies, including 425 of the Fortune 500, the top ten telecommunications companies, the top five accounting firms, all branches of the United States Military and the U.S. Departments of State, Homeland Security, Commerce and Energy, as well as hundreds of universities and colleges worldwide, SolarWinds was the perfect target for hackers: the quintessential single-point-of-failure nexus for a software supply-chain attack.

HACKER

The SolarWinds Orion platform (versions 2019.4 HF 5 through 2020.2.1) that were released between March 2020 and June 2020 were ultimately found to contain a Trojan component (i.e., unwanted computer code that enabled entities outside of SolarWinds to access the systems and devices of users that installed and executed the SolarWinds product). Hackers had modified a platform plug-in, SolarWinds.Orion.Core.BusinessLayer.dll, that had been distributed as part of Orion platform updates by inserting malware. The malware included a "back door" that, when executed by the users' systems and devices, communicated with third-party servers controlled by the attackers.

According to FireEye, "The malware masquerades its network traffic as the Orion Improvement Program (OIP) protocol and stores reconnaissance results within legitimate plugin configuration files allowing it to blend in with legitimate SolarWinds activity. The backdoor uses multiple obfuscated blocklists to identify forensic and anti-virus tools running as processes, services, and drivers."

The small malware program – which was intended to facilitate an extraction attack – was disguised and hidden within thousands of lines of innocent Orion platform code.

As the old saying goes, the best place to hide a grain of sand is on the beach.

Hidden in Plain Sight

What is most concerning about the SolarWinds incident is the fact that software supply-chain attacks like this are nothing new or unexpected. Security experts have been warning for years that software supply-chain attacks are some of the hardest types of cyberattacks to prevent because they take advantage of trusted relationships between vendors and customers, and machine-to-machine communication channels, such as software update mechanisms, that are inherently trusted by users.

A Cautionary Tale

One of the most concerning issues with the SolarWinds hack is that the malware was only detected by a fortunate confluence of circumstances. In other words, it was found by sheer dumb luck.

The SolarWinds attack completely eluded detection by the most sophisticated cybersecurity walls and moats ever created; those developed by the United States Defense, Security and Intelligence Agencies. The collective capabilities of departments and agencies whose combined budgets exceed a few trillion dollars annually not only completely missed this threat, but they also actually unintentionally invited the enemy into their systems.

Size Does Not Always Matter

To put an even finer point on the scale of cyber security investments, here is a partial list of the U.S. government agencies and departments that missed the SolarWinds hack, each of which have millions to billions budgeted to detect and defend against cyberattacks:

Air Force Intelligence

Army Intelligence

Central Intelligence Agency

Coast Guard Intelligence

Cybersecurity and Infrastructure Security Agency

Defense Intelligence Agency

Department of Defense

Department of Energy

Department of Homeland Security

Department of State

Department of the Treasury

Drug Enforcement Administration

Federal Bureau of Investigation

Marine Corps Intelligence

National Geospatial-Intelligence Agency

National Reconnaissance Office

National Security Agency

Navy Intelligence

Space Force Intelligence

United States Cyber Command

Each of the 250+ government agencies and departments that were hit by the SolarWinds hack also have their own Chief Information Security Office (CISO), System Administrators, and IT support. That means that, despite having thousands of professionals on the payroll committed to ensuring cybersecurity, they still saw their safeguards beaten, bypassed, and breached.

Of course, it was not just the government that was caught unaware. The Orion product is an infrastructure monitoring and management platform that is "designed to simplify IT administration." Meaning each of the 18,000+ private company customers were also likely infected make annual investments of hundreds of thousands to millions of dollars in their own IT teams and cybersecurity efforts.

When it comes to keeping your digital assets safe, it's not the size of your budget – it's what you do with it that counts.

Sobering Thought

If your company uses computers and a network to support your operations, if you have a website, if you regularly access services, shop, or even browse online, you are not just a target for cyber-criminals, we can guarantee that in the time it takes you to read this book, at least a few hackers from somewhere around the world will try to make it past your perimeter. More disturbingly, eventually, they will succeed. And you likely won't even know if or when they do.

Advanced Persistent Threats (APT) refer to the latest cyber-scourge. These stealthy cyber-sneaks gain unauthorized access to computer networks and remain undetected for an extended period. APT assaults are typically sponsored by nation states, state-sponsored agencies, and/or collaborative criminal groups. They are well funded, focused, and likely more capable than anyone on your payroll.

Finding Hay in a Haystack

The clue that led to the unravelling of the SolarWinds attack came as the sort of warning most of us get on a regular basis. A FireEye employee received a notice that someone had used his credentials to log into the company's virtual private network from an unrecognized device. This perhaps overly conscientious and diligent employee forwarded the alert he received to the company's security team. Had he not done so, the attack would likely still be undetected; a sobering thought, to say the least.

When Charles Carmakal, Senior Vice President of the Incident Response Unit for FireEye received the report of suspicious activity coming from their own version of the SolarWinds' Orion product, he took the unprecedented step of assigning over 100 of the firm's malware analysts to scour through 50,000 lines of code.

Their mission, as Carmakal said, was to search for a proverbial "needle in a haystack." The cyber-sleuths eventually spotted a few dozen lines of suspicious code that did not appear to have any reason to be there. And those few dozen lines were, upon further analysis, con-firmed to have been the source of the hack.

With all due respect to Carmakal, spotting a few lines of code sur-reptitiously inserted into a file of over 50,000 lines of similar looking code is less like finding a needle in a haystack and more like finding a single stalk of hay that has been carefully camouflaged to look like every other piece of hay in the stack. It is a nearly impossible feat – even for a company with the ability to assign 100 experts to conducting the search.

6

The Enemy in Our Midst

As disturbing as the SolarWinds incident was, it is perhaps even more disturbing to know that this attack was unsurprising. Even expected.

David Kennedy, a former National Security Agency (NSA) hacker and founder of the security consulting firm TrustedSec, said in an interview with CSO magazine, "When you look at what happened with SolarWinds, it's a prime example of where an attacker could literally select any target that has their product deployed, which is a large number of companies from around the world, and most organizations would have no ability to incorporate that into how they would respond from a detection and prevention perspective. This is not a discussion that's happening in security today."

"I just got a friend request
from someone in the castle."

Kennedy went on to say, "While software that is deployed in organizations might undergo security reviews to understand if their developers have good security practices in the sense of patching product vulnerabilities that might get exploited, organizations don't think about how that software could impact their infrastructure if its update mechanism is compromised."

According to Kennedy, "It's something that we're still very immature on and there's no easy solution for it, because companies need software to run their organizations, they need technology to expand their presence and remain competitive, and the organizations that are providing this software don't think about this as a threat model either."

War Gaming

Kennedy contends a starting point should be encouraging software developers to think more about how to protect their code integrity and to consider ways to minimize risks to customers when architecting their products. "A lot of times you know when you're building software, you think of a threat model from outside in, but you don't always think from inside out. That's an area a lot of people need to be looking at: How do we design our architecture infrastructure to be more resilient to these types of attacks? Would there be ways for us to stop a lot of these attacks by minimizing the infrastructure in the [product] architecture?"

Cyber Savvy

The SolarWinds hack – while more sophisticated than most – is emblematic of the increased capabilities being utilized by cybercriminals. As reported in *The Wall Street Journal*, "The hackers used the digital equivalent of a spy's disguise to blend in with the flood of data flowing through government and corporate networks and remain undetected. They snatched up years-old but abandoned internet domains and repurposed them for hacking, and they named their software to mimic legitimate corporate tools. Most devastatingly, they sneaked their malicious code into the legitimate software of a trusted software maker."

The SolarWinds intrusion attack is reminiscent of the extraordinary damage done in 2017 when Russian hackers used an obscure Ukrainian tax program as a transmission vector for a Trojan horse that subsequently metastasized and spread to companies including Merck, Maersk, FedEx, Saint-Gobain, Reckitt Benckiser and Mondelēz, the parent company of Nabisco and Cadbury

In the final tally, the White House approximated that attack, now known as NotPetya, to have caused approximately $10 billion (USD) in damages.

The consensus among cybersecurity professionals is that hacks like SolarWinds and NotPetya are little more than the first puffs of an impending hurricane of epic proportions. The worst is yet to come.

Beat the Clock

A study conducted by the Clark School at the University of Maryland in 2020 reported that a hacker attack now occurs, on average, every 39 seconds. The Federal Bureau of Investigation (FBI) has reported a 300 percent increase in reported cybercrimes since the beginning of the COVID-19 pandemic. The NSA data center in Utah reportedly experiences as many as 300 million hacking attempts every day.

Countdown

Did you know, every:

- 4 minutes a high-risk application is used

- 81 seconds a known malware is downloaded

- 53 seconds a bot calls its command-and-control center

- 30 seconds a threat emulation occurs

- 5 seconds a host accesses a malicious website

- 4 seconds an unknown malware is downloaded

And lest you think small and midsized businesses (SMB) are immune… think again. Because of their relatively lower levels of cybersecurity capabilities, SMBs have become the new target of choice for hackers. And the impact of those attacks can be catastrophic.

According to IBM, the average total cost of a data breach in very large companies (those with more than 25,000 employees) was approximately $4.25 million in 2020; a relative drop in a very big bucket for companies that measure their annual profits in billions. By contrast, much smaller companies (those with 500 employees or fewer) suffered average total costs of data breaches of $2.35 million in 2020.

Is that the sort of hit your company could just shrug off?

Companies Are Left to Fend for Themselves

As if the situation is not dire enough, *The New York Times* has reported there will likely be 3.5 million unfilled cybersecurity jobs globally by 2022 – up from one million positions in 2014. Small and midsized businesses (SMBs) are consequently increasingly being forced to fight a war for rarified (and very expensive) talent.

Making that stat far, far worse, *MIT Technology Review* reports that, "of the candidates who apply, fewer than one in four are even qualified." The Information Systems Security Association (ISSA) likewise reports 61 percent of surveyed companies found their cybersecurity applicants to not be sufficiently qualified.

Given the unprecedented uptick in cybercrime that has accompanied the COVID-19 pandemic, we will likely see the needs for qualified cybersecurity professionals far exceed these expectations.

If you are the CEO of an SMB, you are under siege. So, what do you do?

"What we really need in IT
is someone who has super powers."

7

Storming the Castle

Okay, this may seem like a bit of a departure, but bear with us.

Picture a typical medieval castle, the kind you have read about since you were a kid and have seen in countless movies.

"Our firewall barely protects our content."

What do all castles have in common? They all have layered defenses to repel an attack. Massive walls, drawbridges, moats, gatehouses, and inner walls to redirect traffic. If you study real-life castles you will also find similar features meant to make them virtually impregnable.

Security by the Numbers

Why do you suppose medieval architects didn't simply focus on building very thick and sturdy walls? Because any layer of security, no matter how good, can be breached.

Let's say you have a single line of defense that is 99.9 percent effective. That means, by definition, an average of one out of every one thousand attacks will get through.

But what if you have two lines of defense that are each 99.9 percent effective? Now only one of the one-in-a-thousand of the one-in-a-thousand assaults that make it through that first line of defense can make it through the second. That means only one in a million attacks will make its way through your defenses.

And here's even better news. Add just another three layers and you have reduced your threat exposure to, on average, only one in one hundred trillion of the original assaults being able to get through.

In security circles, this is referred to as a Defense in Depth, or a Concentric Circles of Defense strategy (it also happens to be the meaning behind our logo at ProtectedBy.AI).

The greatest cyber-risk most organizations face is that, rather than implement successive layers of defense, they just dig deeper moats and focus on fortifying their outer walls.

Traditional approaches to cybersecurity are focused on strengthening and thickening walls and digging deeper moats, a perspective that is largely effective at keeping at intruders out. But what do you do when unwittingly these saboteurs are not just allowed, but invited and welcomed in?

It's sad to say, but to keep your organization safe the best perspective is zero trust; a security perspective that requires all users, even insiders, to be authenticated, authorized, and approved – and to continuously be required to validate and re-validate security configuration and credentials before being granted access to applications and data.

The good news is that most of these additional security precautions can be automated, and they impose little to no additional burden on customers, partners, or employees. But even in those instances when this mindset may occasionally add some minor inconvenience, you have to wonder: How much of a hassle do your employees think it is to take the time to lock up and put the petty cash in the safe when they leave the office in the evening? Isn't it worth taking some precautions to keep your company safe?

Zero Trust

In a COVID and Post-COVID world, your employees and customers may expect to be able to access your networks on any type of device and from anywhere in the world. That increased freedom comes with burdens. It means you can no longer just depend on hardening the perimeter of your castle to keep yourself safe.

Zero Trust security requires every person and device that accesses your network to be authenticated through an identity verification process. It's analogous to the evolving experience of air travel.

Remember back in the day when security consisted of walking through a marginally effective metal detector and having the ticket clerk ask if you packed your own bags? Today, the TSA (and their peer agencies around the world) requires you to have a valid and approved ID.

A similar procedure is now required by security-smart companies: the presentation of a secondary valid ID that goes beyond an easily hackable password.

The mindset of Zero Trust is to not let 'just anyone' stroll up to and through the gate. Whether accessing the network from inside or out, anyone wanting access needs to show their verifiable ID. With cybercriminals getting smarter and better every day, you can no longer assume that just because someone has gotten over the moat and through the front door, they are who they say they are.

Later in this book you will read about the next evolution of Zero Trust, Sub-Zero Trust, as implemented through **CodeLock™** – a capability that has been described by the United States Department of Homeland Security (DHS) as being able to "stop the most sophisticated criminal malware."

Trojan Horses

You know the story; it has been told and retold for thousands of years...

The people of Troy had defended themselves for a decade from the Greek army by taking refuge behind walls so impressive that legend had it they had been built by the gods. Poseidon and Apollo, it was said, had been pressed into service to make the city impregnable to any assault.

"I'm nervous about bringing it in the house."

After a decade of frustration, Odysseus, the legendary Greek king of Ithaca and the hero of Homer's epic poem the Odyssey, devised a plan. At his direction, a huge wooden horse was constructed with a secret compartment inside.

The Greeks brought the horse to the city gates and then pretended to sail away. When their ships were out of sight, the Trojans pulled the horse into their city as a victory trophy. That night, Odysseus and his soldiers crept out of the horse and opened the gates for the rest of the Greek army, which had returned under cover of darkness.

The Greeks had bypassed the impregnable walls; they had been invited in. They entered the city and, as their enemies slept, slaughtered, sacked and destroyed the city of Troy.

Beware of Greeks Bearing Gifts

Trojan horse malware disguises itself as innocuous code or software. Once downloaded by unsuspecting users, the Trojan can take control of victims' systems. Trojans can be hidden in games, apps or even delivered as software updates and patches. They can also be embedded in attachments included in emails or as poisonous cookies in websites.

8

The Fault Is Not in Our Stars, But in Ourselves

As King Priam and his son Prince Hector of Troy would be the first to tell you, walls are a necessary but insufficient strategy for repelling invaders.

The same holds true for firewalls in the digital realm.

The Most Wanted List

Network security systems have remained largely unchanged since the 1980s: confirmed and potential threats, when (if) they are identified are logged and recorded. Subsequent visitors are then checked against a blacklist of these known offenders.

The more sophisticated systems do essentially the same thing; with the exception that identification of offenders may be pooled and shared. Some vendors even develop profiles that, in theory, allow the identification of bad actors that bear a resemblance to previous perpetrators.

As any candid cybersecurity professional will tell you, this antiquated approach is like hiring a slow-witted security guard, arming him with a list of undesirables, and asking him to man the velvet rope at your cyber-door.

Think you can't be hacked? Think again. Kevin Mitnick, who was once on the FBI's most wanted list for hacking into more than 40 major corporations (just for the fun of it) now leads an information security firm that boasts a 100 percent success rate of breaking into their clients' systems.

Timing Is Everything

Given the inherent limitations of the approach of these obsolescent approaches, it is little wonder why so many hackers are able to successfully bypass most systems – and why companies take an average of 197 days to detect a data breach.

Unwelcome Guests

While well-constructed firewalls and other breach-preventing capabilities are invaluable to aspects of any security system, the thickest walls and best guards do you no good when the enemy is invited in through the front door. These sorts of attacks are all the more of an affront because they are typically invited in by unsuspecting employees of your own company.

We have all been told hundreds of times to not open email attachments, download software from suspicious sources, plug in that USB drive we found, or even visit questionable websites. Well, human nature being what it is, these sorts of things likely happen in your company at least a few times every day.

"Social engineering" is just a fancy term for conning, tricking, defrauding, lying and psychological manipulation. It is the method hackers use to take advantage of laziness, ignorance, naiveté, gullibility, stupidity

– and most unfortunately, good-natured, well-intentioned, service-oriented trust. They use information they gain from innocent employees to open the gates and invite malware into your system.

Hackers who employ insertion attacks take advantage of the facts that (1) malware can be written in a manner that makes it indistinguishable from the corpus of code into which it is inserted; and (2) commercial software typically relies on thousands to millions of lines of code. Hiding a few lines of camouflaged, innocuous looking malware within massive amounts of otherwise similar looking code makes these cyber-cancers virtually impossible to detect.

Security from Within

From the earliest days of computing, the primary focus of security has been on keeping the bad guys out. But what do you do when the crime has already occurred? When hackers have either breached your defenses or been invited in?

Maintain the Evidentiary Chain

Imagine this: You're a police detective and you respond to the scene of a shooting. When you arrive, you find a spent shell casing lying on the floor. The crime scene technician has already taken photos and now it's up to you. What do you do?

Simple. Being careful not to contaminate the casing or smudge any possible fingerprints, you collect the evidence and secure it in a suitable container. That container is then sealed and signed. The container must be designed to ensure the item cannot be removed without the seal being broken, and the seal also ensures no contaminants can be introduced and the contents of the container cannot be tampered with. Why? Because when the District Attorney asks you, when you're on the stand, if that is the shell you collected, you can testify with certainty that it is.

A chain of custody is established through tracking who had access to that container and where it was stored – and your signature guarantees that the container contains the very same shell you collected.

This same procedure is used by every police agency in the world. Why? Because it's absolutely bulletproof (pardon the pun).

So, why aren't we doing the same thing with computer code? Hold that thought, as we take a slight detour to explain how Blockchain plays into the story.

The Weakest Link

When it comes to cybersecurity, the most exasperating realization for CEOs tends to come from learning that the greatest threats they face may already be on their payroll.

Hackers routinely gain access to networks, data, and systems by preying on employees, vendors, and upstream/downstream business partners who are lazy, gullible, and/or downright dishonest.

Lazy: If you have three or more employees, we can pretty much guarantee at least one of them uses one of the following passwords to access your system: password, qwerty, 111111, abc123, iloveyou, 12345[...]. Where did we get those passwords? They come from Dark Web sites that list the thousands of passwords that are most commonly used. And with just a few lines of computer code, any High School Hacker can check all those passwords against every account connected to your system in a matter of minutes. The worst part? Most people tend to use the same few passwords for everything – both in their professional and personal life. So once the bad guys have the credentials for one account...

Gullible: Social Engineering (in the context of information security) is the use of deception to manipulate individuals into divulging confidential or personal information that may be used for fraudulent purposes. Con, swindle, bamboozle, defraud… Whatever you call it, there have been those who prey on the naiveté of others since Caveman Carl sold Neanderthal Ned the Brooklyn Bridge (selling a bridge before bridges were invented was one hell of a grift!). Over the past few years hoodwinking hackers have become increasingly innovative and have developed scalable scams by setting up websites with enticing offers. All their targets have to do to get the prize? Enter their email and pick any password they like; a password that, these denizens of the Dark Web know, will likely be the same one they use at work.

Thieves: While the vast majority of employees would never even consider stealing from or otherwise harming the company (or country) they have pledged their allegiance to, it only takes one exception to existentially imperil an organization. Why would a person you are paying betray your trust? A considerable body of research has shown there to be three mutually reinforcing factors that collectively contribute to the likelihood an employee will engage in actions that are intended to harm their own organization: Motivation, Opportunity, and Rationalization. Motivation typically comes down to money or revenge for a perceived slight. Opportunity speaks for itself. The trickiest part of the pyramid involves Rationalization; the way in which the perpetrators convince themselves that there (a) is no real harm caused by their actions, (b) the victim got what they deserved, and/or (c) the perpetrator had been treated inequitably or unfairly and their actions merely balanced the scales. Disgruntled and imminently departing employees, company reorganizations and employee reassignments, and granting new employees access to high-value files… These are just a few of the flags that should put a potential threat on your radar.

The U.S. Department of Homeland Security (DHS) suggests that to address insider threats, it is imperative for organizations to develop capabilities in six areas:

- Collect and Analyze (monitoring)
- Detect (provide incentives and data)
- Deter (prevention)
- Protect (maintain operations and economics)
- Predict (anticipate threats and attacks)
- React (reduce opportunity, capability and motivation and morale for the insider bad-actor)

9

Blockchain 101

On October 31, 2008, a paper was published on the cryptography mailing list at metzdowd.com describing a novel idea for a digital cryptocurrency. The paper, *Bitcoin: A Peer-to-Peer Electronic Cash System*, was submitted under the pseudonym Satoshi Nakamoto. No one knows for sure who Nakamoto is (or who they are), but with Bitcoin he/she/they launched a new asset class that now has a collective value across all cryptocurrencies of over $1 trillion.

At the time of this writing, Satoshi Nakamoto has a net worth of around $24 billion. According to Fortune Magazine, that makes Satoshi one of the 100 richest people in the world.

Blockchain Database

That world-changing paper not only created the world's first cryptocurrency, but it also invented the first blockchain database.

A blockchain database holds small amounts of information together in groups, known as blocks. In the case of cryptocurrency transactions, these blocks store basic ledger data: The date and time of a transaction, identifications of the sender and recipient, and the amount included in a record of the transaction are recorded. After several transactions are similarly recorded, the blocks are locked and sealed, and a new block is created and chained to its predecessor.

Did you catch that? The sealed *Blocks* are *Chain*ed together. Blockchain.

Signed, Sealed and Delivered

Blockchains are based on an ingenious bit of computational mathematics known as a Hash Function. The hash function converts any information taken as input and returns a fixed-size string.

As an example, the SHA256 hash function, which is one of the most popular hash functions there is (as evidenced by the fact all the other hash functions want to ask it to the prom) takes whatever information is entered as input and returns an output that is exactly 64 characters long.

If you enter the letter "a" or the letter "A" or the entire contents of Tolstoy's classic novel, *War and Peace* as input into a hash function, it will always output a string of exactly 64 characters. And every time you enter the same data in a hash function, you will get exactly the same 64 characters as output. That means if you change ANYTHING about the input – if you change an upper-case A to a lower-case a… if you remove or add a space to a million lines of text…if you add an extra space between two words, any change will result in a completely different hash value.

If you like, you can try using a hash
function yourself by going to: bit.ly/TrySHA256

The hash function is at the core of blockchain – and it is an essential element of the most revolutionary development ever invented for combatting intrusion attacks: **CodeLock™**

10

CodeLock™

Putting the concepts that we have presented together – insertion attacks, blockchain, algorithms, hash functions, and methods for securing evidence by affixing seals and signatures to containers – you now have essentially all the elements you need to understand CodeLock™.

CodeLock™ is a patent-pending process that was developed by ProtectedBy.AI. This revolutionary approach provides what the Department of Homeland Security (DHS) describes as being able to "stop the most sophisticated criminal malware."

The CodeLock™ algorithm inserts specialized "digital signatures" at predetermined locations throughout an entire body of code, effectively creating containers of code that are then sealed, signed and linked together.

Through this simple process, CodeLock™ creates an inviolable network of security sensors that can be embedded into any software running on your servers. Returning to the castle metaphor: CodeLock™ puts alarms on every window, door and room. If any malware or unexpected code is introduced into the software your organization depends on, CodeLock™ sounds the alarm and locks hackers out.

How It Works

The digital signatures appended to each code container are successively linked in a hash chain. This creates a mutually reinforcing and tamper-proof blockchain-type structure that instantly discloses any unauthorized additions, deletions, or changes to the protected code in each of the blocks.

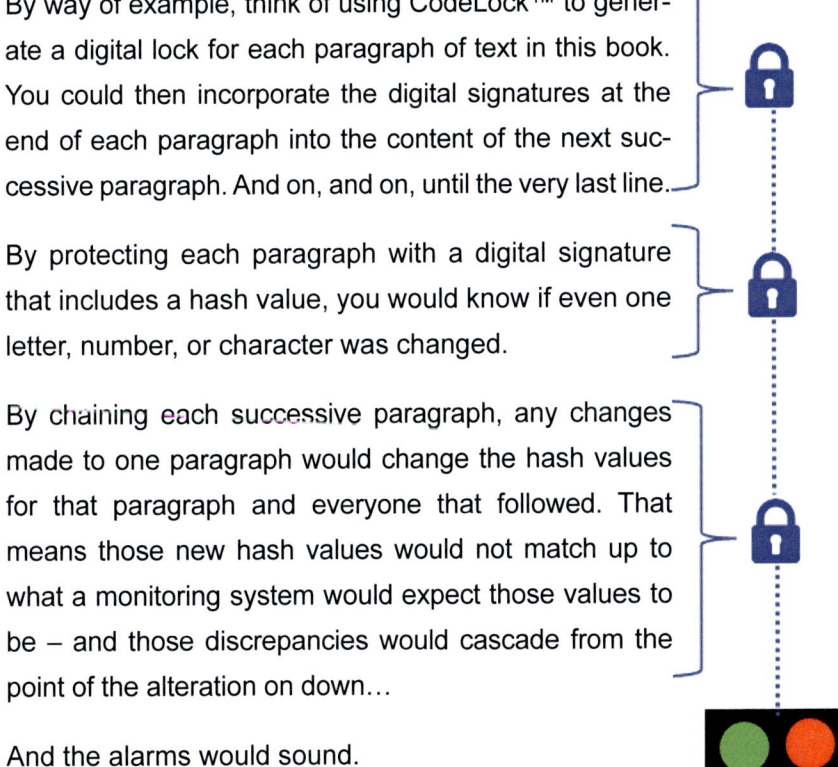

By way of example, think of using CodeLock™ to generate a digital lock for each paragraph of text in this book. You could then incorporate the digital signatures at the end of each paragraph into the content of the next successive paragraph. And on, and on, until the very last line.

By protecting each paragraph with a digital signature that includes a hash value, you would know if even one letter, number, or character was changed.

By chaining each successive paragraph, any changes made to one paragraph would change the hash values for that paragraph and everyone that followed. That means those new hash values would not match up to what a monitoring system would expect those values to be – and those discrepancies would cascade from the point of the alteration on down...

And the alarms would sound.

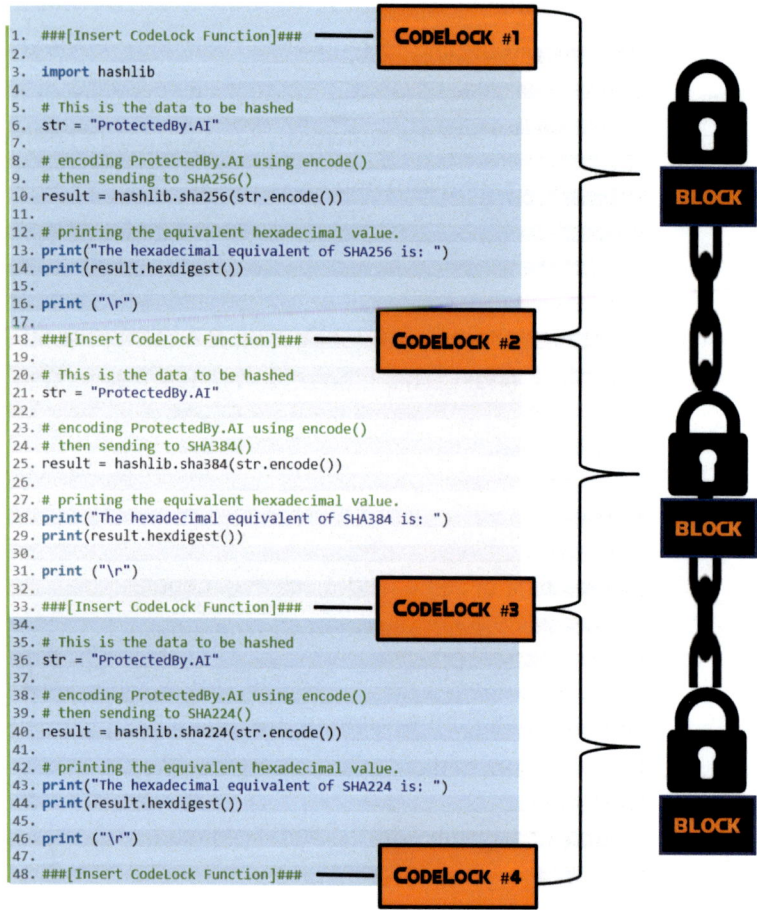

```
1.  ###[Insert CodeLock Function]###
2.
3.  import hashlib
4.
5.  # This is the data to be hashed
6.  str = "ProtectedBy.AI"
7.
8.  # encoding ProtectedBy.AI using encode()
9.  # then sending to SHA256()
10. result = hashlib.sha256(str.encode())
11.
12. # printing the equivalent hexadecimal value.
13. print("The hexadecimal equivalent of SHA256 is: ")
14. print(result.hexdigest())
15.
16. print ("\r")
17.
18. ###[Insert CodeLock Function]###
19.
20. # This is the data to be hashed
21. str = "ProtectedBy.AI"
22.
23. # encoding ProtectedBy.AI using encode()
24. # then sending to SHA384()
25. result = hashlib.sha384(str.encode())
26.
27. # printing the equivalent hexadecimal value.
28. print("The hexadecimal equivalent of SHA384 is: ")
29. print(result.hexdigest())
30.
31. print ("\r")
32.
33. ###[Insert CodeLock Function]###
34.
35. # This is the data to be hashed
36. str = "ProtectedBy.AI"
37.
38. # encoding ProtectedBy.AI using encode()
39. # then sending to SHA224()
40. result = hashlib.sha224(str.encode())
41.
42. # printing the equivalent hexadecimal value.
43. print("The hexadecimal equivalent of SHA224 is: ")
44. print(result.hexdigest())
45.
46. print ("\r")
47.
48. ###[Insert CodeLock Function]###
```

CODELOCK #1

CODELOCK #2

CODELOCK #3

CODELOCK #4

BLOCK

BLOCK

BLOCK

It doesn't take a graduate degree in Computer Science to see where the insertion attack occurred. Which would mean, in this case, your IT team could go right to the Block protected by CodeLock™ 6:

Technically Speaking

Fair Warning: This section includes a bit of geek-speak

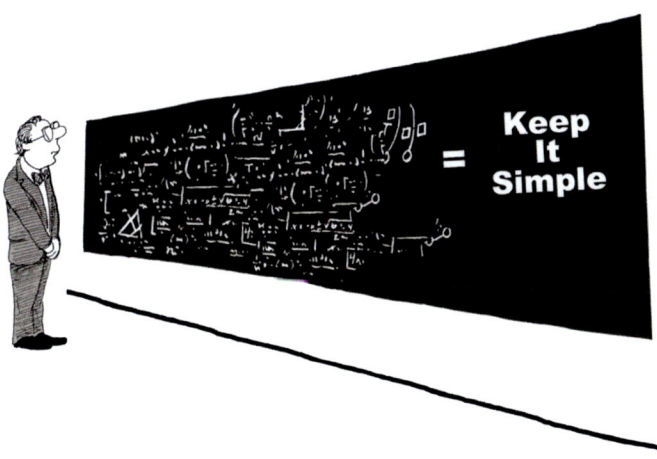

By dynamically generating hash values and appending them to each block of code – and incorporating the function call for doing so within the corpus of code being hashed – it becomes impossible for hackers or other malicious actors (even if they are somehow able to somehow divine and then forge a digital signature so that it appears genuine) to insert that static, forged line of code in place of the proper function.

Because the CodeLock™ function is incorporated into the generated hash value, each block becomes inextricably linked to the contents of the container of code as well as the hash value from the preceding blocks and the CodeLock™ function call. If any changes are made to any of these three elements, the hash value becomes corrupted and is revealed to have been tampered with.

By incorporating a unique hash value into the digital signature, if even one character contained within a block of code is changed in any way, the hash value changes. That means even if a tainted open-source library is integrated into the codebase, as soon that bit of malware begins to metastasize or alter the code in any way, the CodeLock™ monitoring system will record that change and issue an alert.

The CodeLock™ digital signatures are inserted into the code as non-executable comments, effectively rending these digital signatures invisible to the flow of the program into which they are embedded. The embedded digital signatures consequently do not interfere with the operation of the underlying code into which the digital signatures are inserted, and they effectively operate as a meta-program that wraps the functional codebase.

While digital signatures have historically been limited by their reliance on a trusted intermediary, the CodeLock™ approach emulates several of the features that make blockchain algorithms so formidable and have led to their wide adoption. By incorporating an interface that supports the successive linking of dynamically generated hash values into a publicly disclosable interface for reporting the digital signatures, CodeLock™ also incorporates the blockchain features of decentralization, immutability, nonrepudiation, trustless security and transparency for the protected code.

Defense Mechanism

The CodeLock™ algorithm is configured by the user to dynamically insert digital signatures at particular locations within target code by inserting function calls to generate digital signatures that are linked in a blockchain-type structure (e.g., a hash chain) at particular locations within the target code.

For example, if the target code includes 100 lines of code and the computing device is configured to insert digital signatures after every 10 lines of code, the computing device may insert a first digital signature function call at line 0, then a second after line 10 of the target code and a third digital signature function call after line 20 of the target code, continuing until the end.

In this example, the first digital signature function call may be configured to enable generation of a first digital signature (e.g., a first hash value), then a second digital signature based on a combination of lines 1-10 of the target code and the first two digital signature function calls, and the third digital signature function call may be configured to enable generation of a third digital signature (e.g., a second hash value) based on a combination of lines 11-20 of the target code, the third, second, and first digital signature function calls. Additional digital signature function calls may be similarly inserted in target code that includes as many lines of code as the user specifies and/or after particular object definitions, class definitions, functions, loops, function calls, or the like.

Matched Set

If CodeLock™ digital signatures do not match the digital signatures received from the computing device (or stored at another location, such as a code database), alarms sound and reports are generated showing when the monitored code has been tampered with and where it has been corrupted.

11

Parting Thoughts

Technologies developed over the past few years have contributed to historically unprecedented opportunities. Companies that were once bound to a single geography have been liberated to serve global markets. Efficiencies and capabilities that were once only available to the fortunate few in the Fortune 500 can now be accessed by even the smallest mom-and-pop shops. To remain competitive, businesses in every industry and sector must now become digitally enabled and data driven.

The opportunities technology presents are now borderless, boundless and based on the ability to capitalize on the new gold of the modern economy – which are all stored on servers in zeros and ones.

But whenever there are opportunities to be gained, there are those who will take advantage of those who leave their assets exposed. Along with the unprecedented opportunities presented by technology, organizations of every size are now having to contend with new hazards and risks. Chief among those challenges: Keeping the data that drives our organizations safe has now become everyone's business.

A robust approach to keeping your data assets safe requires the development and deployment of a holistic suite of solutions that can interdict, detect, and defeat attacks. Cybersecurity also requires a shift in the cultural mindset that requires every employee to consider themselves to be a data fiduciary; a perspective and example that must begin at the top.

CEOs and senior executives can no longer abrogate their responsibility for cybersecurity to IT, or even a CISO. For nearly every organization, data has become at least as important as any other asset. And keeping those assets safe are a primary part of every executive's responsibility.

The information contained in this short book has, we hope, made you a bit more aware of the dangers you face and the resources at your disposal to keep your organization safe.

What you do with this information, however, is entirely up to you.

If you need help, if you want advice… even if you just want someone to yell to about how damn difficult tech has made your life, we will look forward to hearing from you – before we hear about you in the press.

JT & Brian

Peace of Mind Through Superior Technology©

Thanks to recent advances in technology, it is now possible for you to effectively (and cost-effectively) outsource all your cyber-security concerns. To ensure you don't lose sleep stressing about what will happen when you are (inevitably) hacked, ProtectedBy. AI can provide everything you need to safeguard your data assets.

Our security related services include:

- **Assessments** – Risk Assessments, Gap Analyses, and Penetration Testing provide invaluable insights into where you are – and where you need to be.

- **>SOC** – A Virtual Security Operations Center that pro-vides a turnkey state-of-the-art 24/7 monitoring solution to meet all your cybersecurity needs – for a fraction of the cost of even entry-level IT team members (let alone the salaries and expenses that come with maintaining a team of crack cybersecurity experts in-house as employees on your payroll).

- **SmartShield** – For companies and countries contending with sophisticated Advanced Persistent Threats (APT) by state actors and organized hackers, we deploy a suite of customized AI-enabled capabilities originally designed for the U.S. Intelligence Community that can integrate into your existing security operations environment.

- **SmartChain** – A fully encrypted, tamper-proof, block-chain-based AI-enabled supply chain management sys-tem that gives you the ability to instantly trace and track every package, parcel, part, and product from the point of production.

- **DataLock3r** – A fully secured virtual vault for storing and transferring sensitive files and digital data. With five levels of impregnable security this drag-and-drop user-friendly solution is as simple to use as it is secure.

- **CodeLock™** – A newly developed patent-pending game-changing capability described by the United States Department of Homeland Security (DHS) as being able to "stop the most sophisticated criminal malware."

- **ReAbled Veterans** – An on-site or virtual team of Honorably Discharged Disabled Veterans of the U.S. Military who we train with the cybersecurity knowledge, skills and abilities needed to serve and protect your organization.

- **Cyber, Physical, and Procedural Security Assessments, Penetration Testing and Training**

- **Retained, On-Call, or Virtual Chief Information Security Officer (CISO)**

CodeLock™ Features

CodeLock™ incorporates several key features that heighten security:

- **CodeLock™** integrates nonrepudiation by ascribing verifiable credentials to all users authorized to update, change, or otherwise modify any aspect of an overall corpus, or any constituent corpora, of code. For example, any creation or modification of code may be signed based at least in part on credentials of the user responsible for the creation or modification, thereby providing transparency and nonrepudiation of authors of the code. The digital signatures are likewise coded to incorporate datetime stamps and any relevant provenance information through referenced records.

- **CodeLock™** supports verification without dependence on third parties, thereby increasing security and reducing or negating the possibility of interception and man-in-the-middle (MitM) attacks. For example, digital signatures associated with software may be provided to all recipients to enable verification of the authenticity of the software by the recipients. Additionally, or alternatively, the system described herein may utilize a decentralized platform (e.g., decentralized securing and storing of code), which may provide instantaneous/near-instantaneous vetting capabilities to an unlimited number of authorized users.

- **CodeLock™** digital signatures support configurable layers of transparency. For example, authorized users can be provided with access to the underlying codebase, the digital signature, and/or a binary yes/no report on the integrity of digital signature matches. The information provided to each user may be based on the user's authorization level or credentials, thereby supporting configurable transparency to different types of users.

- **CodeLock™** enables instant (e.g., real-time or near-real-time) and continuous auditability. For example, discrepancies between the distributed digital signatures and digital signatures generated by one or more nodes may be identified upon receipt of the code and generation of the digital signatures at the one or more nodes. The chaining nature of the digital signature structure may instantly disclose nodes along the chain which have been corrupted (e.g., received code which has been tampered with, resulting in different digital signature(s)).

- **CodeLock™** supports a "smart contract" capability, which can be incorporated into business processes and procedures. For example, similar to blockchains, the digital signature data structure utilized by the system operates as a smart contract by enabling secure and transparent sharing of digital signatures that are immutable once added to the digital signature data structure.

Glossary

Geek to Plain-Speak Dictionary

APT (Advanced Persistent Threat): Do you remember that movie *When a Stranger Calls*? Spoiler alert: The calls were coming from inside the house! The cyber-equivalent occurs when an attacker infiltrates your system, and then sets up house and camps out. This insidious approach to infecting networks enables attackers to gain access or control over a system for an extended period of time. And you usually don't know they're there until it's too late.

Botnet: Hacking into a computer is a crime. But imagine what might happen if someone were able to coopt dozens, or even millions, of innocent computers and turn them into their own private r*obot network*? Cyber-puppet-masters insert malware into otherwise innocent computers and then use those compromised machines to host false and criminal websites, eavesdrop on and record network communications, spoof websites and send spam, steal passwords and crack encryption, and/or otherwise enable a criminal enterprise. The power of botnets comes from their ability to remain undetected on computers like yours, for years.

Cookie: Mom told us to never take candy and cookies from strangers. Yet most of us do just that every day. Computer cookies are tiny little files that are sent to and stored on your computer every time you visit a website. These little bits of computer code are used to track, target, and retarget you with offers and customized content as you wander around the World Wide Web.

DDoS (Distributed Denial of Service) Attack: Imagine if you had only one main door into your company and all customers were required to enter through that same door. If someone wanted to interfere with your business, they could hire thousands of people to que up in front of that door and force customers to wait in that long, long line. A Denial-of-Service attack takes a similar approach. The attacker continually pings and attempts to access your system, forcing legitimate traffic to wait in line. A DDoS takes a Denial-of-Service several steps further by leveraging the combined forces of numerous computers, all coordinated to attack the same target. DDoS attacks often employ botnet armies of zombies. Think of it as a cyber-version of an episode of *The Walking Dead* – all lined up and trying to access your website. And, of course, eat your brain.

Firewall: In most organizations, this tends to be the first, best, and (unfortunately) only means of defense against cybercriminals. Firewalls filter network traffic, acting as the digital equivalent of a brawny bouncer who checks anyone trying to get into the club against a list. Advanced versions of firewalls can make decisions to let traffic in or keep it out based on user authentication, pre-established protocols, payload contents, and a host of additional factors. The most advanced types of firewalls use Machine Learning to evolve and become smarter and smarter over a relatively short time.

Geek: Originally a slang term used to describe guys who got shoved into their own school lockers, this is now the preferred honorific of computer experts and enthusiasts around the globe. Ever since the 1980s when the Geek God Bill Gates (blessed be his name) burst onto the scene, the most popular meme definition of the term has become:

Geek (*noun*) The person you picked on in high school and ended up working for as an adult.

Hacker: This may well be the most misused technology term of all time. In the original definition, a hacker was any computer expert who used their technical knowledge to achieve a goal or overcome an obstacle by non-standard means (one of the authors of this book was, and is, a hacker). The original definition of 'hacker' was simply someone smart enough and skilled enough to find shortcuts and not have to follow a map or an established path. Tim Berners-Lee, Beto O'Rourke, Linus Torvalds, Steve Wozniak… Hackers, one and all. The term that was originally proposed for bad guys who used their skills in pursuit of not just mischievous but malevolent goals was "cracker." But you can't argue with someone who buys ink by the barrel, so we've all come to accept that hackers are the denizens of the Dark Web who do bad deeds – though those in the know continue to at least make the distinction between White Hat, Grey Hat, and Black Hat Hackers, based on their goals (the author in question has spent 50+ years sporting various shades of grey).

Insider Threat: What's even more infuriating than becoming the victim of cybercrime? Finding out you've been paying the thief who is ripping you off! Employees, vendors and business partners who have been granted access to your systems don't have to circumvent your security; you are already inviting these enemies into your midst. The FBI, CISA, and Interpol warn that Insiders are the most insidious and dangerous threat most organizations face. The Capital One breach that cost the company $150 million? The theft of 41 million customer payment card accounts at Target? The Panama Papers? Edward Snowden? All these attacks – and millions more – were perpetrated by Insiders.

IoT (Internet of Things): Here's something to think about: Your washing machine and watch likely have more computing power than was in the Apollo 11 space capsule that landed on the moon. Computers are now in everything and everywhere. IoT refers to the vast and rapidly expanding network of physical objects that have sensors, software and communication technologies integrated and embedded for the purpose of connecting, sharing and exchanging data with other devices and systems over the internet. IoT brings incredible new opportunities – along with unprecedented security exposure and new risks.

Keylogger: Also known as keystroke logging or keyboard capturing, this hack attack will be sure to give you the creeps. As you type, click, move your mouse or interact in any way with your computer, your actions can be covertly recorded and seen by a cyber-spy who has uploaded a small bit of code to your computer or network. The worst part? Keylogger programs have been around since the 1970s when they were routinely used in the Soviet Union – and they have become so simple, inexpensive and ubiquitous they can now be purchased pre-packaged and sent and used by a child. Want to really feel that chill up your spine? Your IT team may be running a keylogger on the computer you are using right now. For perfectly legitimate purposes, of course, they may be capturing and recording everything you write, receive, send, do and view on your laptop and online. Maybe that's something you should ask them about?

Logic Bomb: Tick, tick, tick. Can you hear it? Probably not. A logic bomb is a piece of malicious code intentionally inserted into your system that is set to go off when specified conditions are met. It could go off at a preset date and time. It could be set to start the second you open that file for the second time. It could begin deleting every single file in your system exactly 42 days and 42 minutes after a former employee was terminated from your company. Tick, tick, tick.

Malware: From the Latin, *wannasmashus mycomputeris* (okay, it's actually a portmanteau of the words *mali*cious and soft*ware*), malware is any software intentionally designed to cause damage to a computer, server, or computer network. Malware comes in more flavors than Baskin Robbins and its ugly incarnations include viruses, worms, Trojan horses, ransomware, spyware, adware, wipers and scareware (seriously…scareware).

Multi-Factor Authentication: When you use your ATM card to get cash or buy groceries, you swipe your card and then enter a PIN. When you access some websites, you are prompted to swipe your fingerprint or enter a number you receive via text. Any system that requires you to provide two or more inputs to verify that you are who you claim to be before giving you access to a resource – an application, online account, VPN or building – is using two-factor, or multi-factor, authentication.

Nonrepudiation: Did you ever hear the expression, "signed in blood?" The legal equivalent for that kind of undeniability is nonrepudiation. It is technically defined as a situation in which an author of a document, statement, record, or action cannot dispute that he or she was the author. In the case of databases and computer systems, metadata with identifying information on the accessing individual is captured and indelibly linked to every data-related interaction, transaction and action.

Penetration Testing: Penetration testing, pen testing, pentesting, ethical or white hat hacking. Whatever you call it, it means the same thing. Your company hires hackers who have the same skills and use the same tools as bad guys who are intent on causing you harm. Why hire a pen tester? Because the best way to prepare to defend against an attack is to defend against an attack.

Phishing: Your Visa has been compromised! Please follow this link, login with your old password and choose a new one. Thank you for providing us with that information. Sucker. Social engineering attacks like this are launched millions of times every day through emails, text messages, social networks, and smart phone apps. When criminals combine their con with a spoof, unsuspecting victims can be tricked into believing they are simply complying with a legitimate request to keep themselves safe. Phishing attacks are often used to obtain logon credentials, credit card information, passwords and personally identifying information (PII).

Ransomware: On June 27, 2017, an IT support technician working at the headquarters of A.P. Møller-Maersk received an ominous message on his computer: "oops, your important files are encrypted". The price to decrypt those files: $300 worth of bitcoin. Annoying, of course. But $300? Such a trivial amount was not worth fretting about. Pay the ransom and get on with your day. If only it had been that simple. The ransom was a ruse and only led to further infections. By the time the NotPetya ransomware virus ran its course, it cost companies – including Maersk, Merck, Mondelēz, FedEx and Reckitt Benckiser, a collective $10 billion (USD). Over the past few years, ransomware has become so rampant and prevalent among SMBs that most (perhaps all) cybersecurity professionals have come to agree: It's no longer a matter of if you will be hit, but when.

Retargeting: Don't you hate it when you search for a pair of tennis shoes or check out a pair of trainers in an online catalog – and then those kicks start to show up and follow you wherever you go? Behavioral retargeting is a form of online targeted advertising that uses information obtained from cookies and tracking pixels to send targeted ads to consumers based on their previous online actions. It really makes you think twice before you visit certain sites. Or maybe that's just us.

SIEM (Security Information and Event Management): Think of a SIEM as a cyber security guard that never takes time off or sleeps. The SIEM is part of a process that ensures the security of your organization is monitored and evaluated on a constant basis, 24/7/365. The SIEM can automatically identify systems that do not comply with security policies and can be configured to notify your IRT (Incident Response Team) of any security violating events. SIEMS never sleep – so you can.

Social Engineering: This is just a fancy term for conning, tricking, defrauding, lying and psychological manipulation. It is the method hackers use to take advantage of laziness, ignorance, naiveté, gullibility, stupidity – and most unfortunately, good-natured, well-intentioned, service-oriented trust. They use information they gain from innocent employees to open the gates and invite malware into your system.

Spoofing: Your phone rings and the caller ID says the call is coming from the FBI. The caller tells you that you owe $5,000 in back taxes – and if you don't give them your credit card number now, agents will be at your house within the hour. Congratulations. You are now one of the millions of victims of an attempted con enabled by a spoof. With algorithms that can be purchased on the dark net for just a few dollars, criminals conceal their identities and disguise themselves as whomever they like. That call you thought was coming from your IT support? It's really from a cybercriminal in the Crimea. Spoofing can be used with phone calls, emails and websites – so *caveat emptor.*

Spyware: This malware does exactly what you think; it monitors user activities and reports the information it collects back to headquarters. Primarily used by hackers to surreptitiously gather data, spyware is also used for more "legitimate" purposes by advertisers and marketers interested in gathering demographic, psychographic and online behavioral data of potential customers… because no one minds the idea of Google, Facebook and Target knowing more about you than your best friend does.

SQL Injection: If your company keeps anything in a database – contact information, inventory or production data, financial records – basically anything kept on a computer – your IT team is almost certainly using a domain-specific computer language known as Structured Query Language (SQL). And if you are using SQL, with just a few lines of computer code hackers may be able to gain access to your entire computer network through your website. How's that for a bit of infuriating irony? Unless you are taking sufficient security precautions, the very same systems you are using to enable and empower your employees, and the capabilities you are paying for to provide service to your customers, may serve as an open door and welcome mat that invites cybercriminals into your inner digital sanctum.

State Actor: A person or group acting on behalf of a government or government body. State-based actors are supported by the government they represent. They may be either declared and overt (e.g., military, diplomatic functionaries, etc.) or they may be covert (e.g., intelligence agencies, sponsored hacker groups, etc.).

Tracking Pixel: Also known as a web beacon, you likely encounter these little beasties several times every day. The more innocuous versions are embedded in web pages and emails to unobtrusively check if a user has accessed some content. If you have ever sent or received a "read receipt" on an email or been retargeted for an ad…welcome to the club. Tracking pixels are commonly used to monitor the activity of website visitors and are embedded into most CRM systems. And while it may be hard to believe that something so mundane and so commonly used can ruin your day, it most certainly can. With a bit of code contained in a single pixel (which is smaller than the period at the end of this sentence), a clever hacker can begin to collect data they can use to exploit you in a matter of minutes. And it's perfectly legal.

Trojan: Trojan horse malware disguises itself as innocuous code or software. Once downloaded by unsuspecting users, the Trojan can take control of victims' systems. Trojans can be hidden in games, apps or even delivered as software updates and patches. They can also be embedded in attachments included in emails or as poisonous cookies in websites.

Virus: These bits and bytes of cancerous computer code are injected into unsuspecting host machines where they metastasize and infect other files. Once they have spread, viruses are virtually impossible to extricate. In most cases the only way to contend with a virus is to quarantine and delete the files it has infected. Much like their biological equivalents hijack healthy cells, viruses parasitically embed themselves into other applications. When the infected applications are then run, the virus is launched and does its damage.

VPN (Virtual Private Network): Computer networks, whether just the tiny little network you may have in your home, or the network known as the internet, allow computers to communicate with one another and share resources, data and applications. A VPN is a secured, private, encrypted communication link between computers, systems or networks that provides a private pathway for communications. A VPN is like having your own private secured road on the information superhighway.

Worm: Perhaps the most onomatopoetically appropriately named malware, worms do just what you would think they do. These nasty little buggers burrow their way into computer networks. Then, just like their hermaphroditic biological namesakes, they self-replicate and spread. If one of your employees opens an infected email attachment, the worm can turn your entire system into swiss cheese in seconds. The notorious *SQL Slammer* worm, which exploited a vulnerability in a popular Microsoft product, spread to every SQL server around the world that was connected to the internet – in under 10 minutes.

Zombie: Mythological undead corporeal revenants that are created through either (a) the magical reanimation of a corpse, or (b) by imbibing in too many tequila shots over the weekend. With respect to computers, this refers to the process of turning a computer into a node in a botnet. Much like their cinematic counterparts, they are mindless minions of evil that thrive on eating your brain.

About the Authors

JT Kostman, PhD
Co-Founder, ProtectedBy.AI

Dr. Kostman has been recognized by his peers, the press, and professional associations as one of the world's leading experts in Applied Artificial Intelligence and Cognitive Computing. A highly sought-after speaker, writer, and advisor, JT has earned a reputation for his ability to demystify frontier technologies, and for developing practical, actionable, cost-efficient data solutions.

In the public sector, JT has hunted terrorists for U.S. Intelligence Agencies, tracked criminal networks for the FBI, advised on analytic strategies for the Department of Defense, and led social media analysis for the 2012 Obama Campaign. In his earlier life, he served as a paramedic, police officer, deep-sea rescue diver, and team leader with the U.S. Army Special Forces.

In the corporate sector, JT led the development of industry-changing solutions while serving as Chief Data Officer for Time Inc., Chief Data Scientist for Samsung, and as an advisor to organizations ranging from tech startups to the Fortune 500.

In the financial sector, JT has guided substantial investments in frontier technologies while serving as a Board Member of a PE/VC fund and as an advisor to numerous hedge funds, family offices, and institutional investors.

In the marketplace of ideas, JT has become one of the most prolific, prescient, and valued voices on the near-term impact of AI and frontier technologies. The keynotes, presentations, press interviews, posts, and articles he has shared with audiences around the world have contributed to making him a go-to expert for organizations including The National Association of Corporate Directors, The Chicago Council on Global Affairs, U.S. Government Agencies, and dozens of others.

Brian J. Gallagher, MPS
Co-Founder, ProtectedBy.AI

Brian Gallagher is widely regarded as a leader and international expert on protecting people, property, places – and profits. Brian has served as an adviser to corporations and countries around the world and is widely considered to be a trailblazer within the fields of security and risk mitigation.

In the public sector, Brian served in the U.S. Secret Service Technical Security Division under U.S. Presidents George W. Bush and Barack Obama. While working in the White House, Brian's remit was focused on new and emerging technologies, with a particular focus on chemical, biological, radiological, nuclear and explosive threats. His expertise has since extended to include the intersection of physical and cybersecurity threats and the hazards they present to governments and private organizations.

In the corporate sector, Brian has worked with customers around the world introducing advanced technology and has become a trusted strategic advisor to CXOs, Senior Executives, and Government Officials. He has established offices and has led teams in North America, Asia and the Middle East.

Brian is a member of the U.S. Chamber of Commercial (USCC) National Security Task Force and serves as an advisor to several government committees. His work focuses on helping public and private sector clients increase their efficiencies and capabilities, while simultaneously reducing their risk through the strategic application of leading-edge technology.

Brian is a highly sought-after speaker, advisor and teacher. He has lectured, interviewed and led workshops in 37 countries. From Presidents and Ministers to industry leaders, Brian has influenced thinking and has helped make companies and countries safer and better prepared to meet tomorrow's challenges – today.

ProtectedBy.AI is the world leader in developing solutions that are at the intersection of Technology and Psychology.

Our comprehensive approach simultaneously addresses Strategic, Human Capital, Insight and Technology needs through the use of a suite of customizable modules created in the course of developing innovative solutions for organizations ranging from Samsung to the CIA; the White House to the United Nations; Time Inc. to tech startups in Silicon Valley, New York, India, Africa and Australia.

The capabilities we develop are powered by ongoing advances the members of our team continue to make in:

Artificial Intelligence, Machine Learning, Deep Learning, Natural Language Processing, Cognitive Computing, Computer Vision, Blockchain and Smart Contracts, IoT Analytics, Intelligent Process Automation, Cybersecurity and Behavioral Data Science.

ProtectedBy.AI provides unparalleled capabilities in: Data Analysis, Logistics, Operations, Consumer Insights, Healthcare and Wellness, National/Corporate Security, Defense, Intelligence, Investigations, Cybersecurity, Safety and Case Management.

www.ProtectedBy.AI
info@ProtectedBy.AI
1-844-4-We-Are-AI